T0199071

My A-B-C Book

Valentina Davenport

Copyright © 2023 Valentina Davenport.

All rights reserved. No part of this book may be used or reproduced by any means, graphic, electronic, or mechanical, including photocopying, recording, taping or by any information storage retrieval system without the written permission of the author except in the case of brief quotations embodied in critical articles and reviews.

WestBow Press books may be ordered through booksellers or by contacting:

WestBow Press
A Division of Thomas Nelson & Zondervan
1663 Liberty Drive
Bloomington, IN 47403
www.westbowpress.com
844-714-3454

Because of the dynamic nature of the Internet, any web addresses or links contained in this book may have changed since publication and may no longer be valid. The views expressed in this work are solely those of the author and do not necessarily reflect the views of the publisher, and the publisher hereby disclaims any responsibility for them.

Any people depicted in stock imagery provided by Getty Images are models, and such images are being used for illustrative purposes only.
Certain stock imagery © Getty Images.

ISBN: 979-8-3850-0223-8 (sc)
ISBN: 979-8-3850-0224-5 (e)

Library of Congress Control Number: 2023915668

Print information available on the last page.

WestBow Press rev. date: 10/19/2023

WESTBOW
PRESS®
A DIVISION OF THOMAS NELSON
& ZONDERVAN

My
A - B - C
Book

Apple

A is for

Alligator

A is for

Bird

B is for

Ball

B is for

Cat

C is for

Cake

C is for

Dog

D is for

Door

D is for

Elephant

E is for

Egg

E is for

Fish

F is for

Fox

F is for

Girl

G is for

Grapes

G is for

Hat

H is for

Horse

H is for

Igloo

I is for

Ice

I is for

Jar

J is for

Jacket

J is for

Kite

K is for

Keys

K is for

Lion

L is for

Lamp

L is for

Mouse

M is for

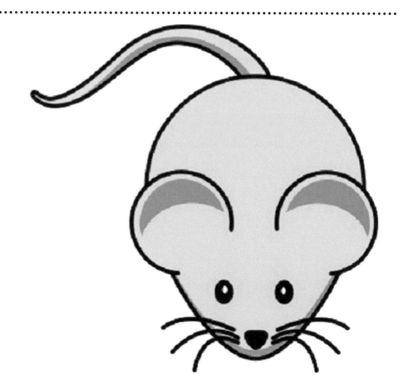

Mask

M is for

Nose

N is for

Nuts

N is for

Orange

O is for

Octopus

O is for

Pearls

P is for

Pencil

P is for

Queen

Q is for

Quilt

Q is for

Rainbow

R is for

Ring

R is for
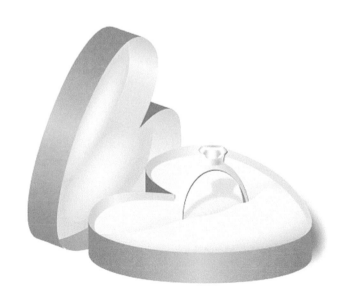

Sun

S is for

Scissors

S is for

Tiger

T is for

Table

T is for

Umbrella

U is for

Unicorn

U is for

Van

V is for

Violin

V is for

Whale

W is for

Watch

W is for

Xylophone

X is for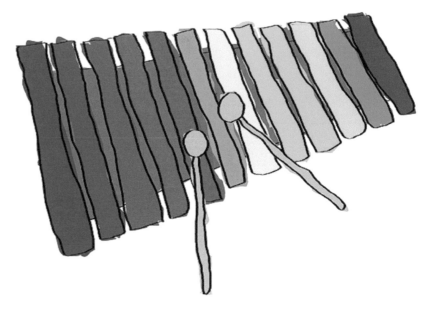

x-ray

X is for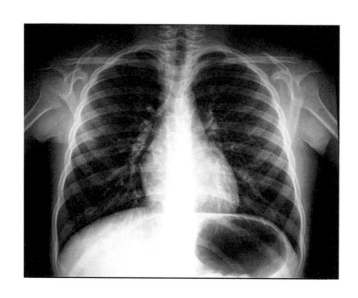

Yellow

Y is for

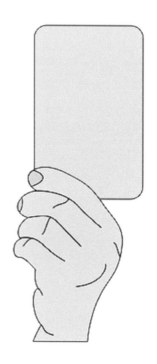

Yarn

Y is for

Zebra

Z is for

Zipper

Z is for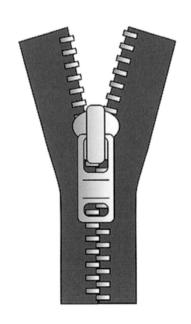

Directions: Look at each picture and write the letter the picture begins with on the line.

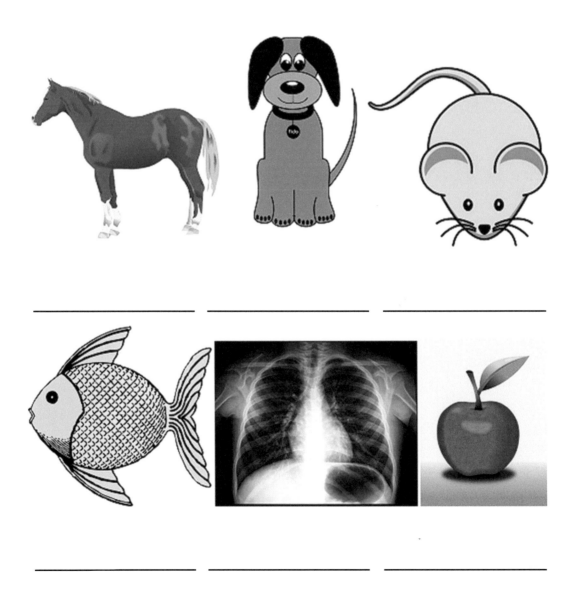

_____ _____ _____

_____ _____ _____

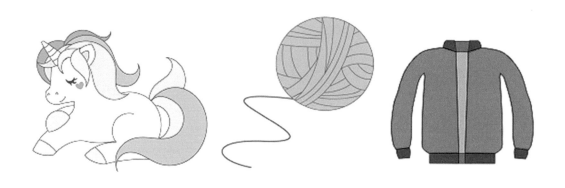

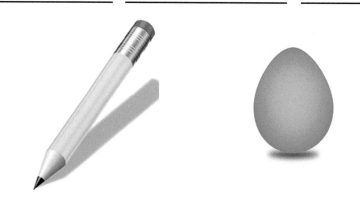

Author Biography

Valentina Davenport is a graduate of Lee University in Cleveland, Tennessee. She is passionate about advocating for children. Her personal style emphasizes building strong foundational skills and prepares them for success.

Printed in the United States
by Baker & Taylor Publisher Services